WELCOME

The Imperial War Museum was founded in 1917 to record the impact of war on individual people — service personnel and civilians alike. Today, across our five branches, we continue to do the same, telling the stories of men, women and children who have been affected by any war involving Britain or the Commonwealth since 1914.

IWM North brings a unique power to these stories, a power woven into the very architecture of the museum itself. Unlike any of our other branches, IWM North is purpose-built to set the scene for the stories within.

Every rivet and girder, every curve and angle is designed to bring a uniquely physical dimension to your experience — exciting and surprising at one turn, challenging and perhaps even unsettling at another.

It is a dimension that lends impact to the stories behind every item on display — every photograph, diary and letter, every flag, medal, uniform and weapon. And it provides the perfect backdrop for the uniquely immersive and interactive displays of sight, sound, touch and even smell that you will find inside.

IWM North offers you an experience that you won't forget. We hope that you find it inspiring, and that you will come back to visit us again soon.

Ground Level

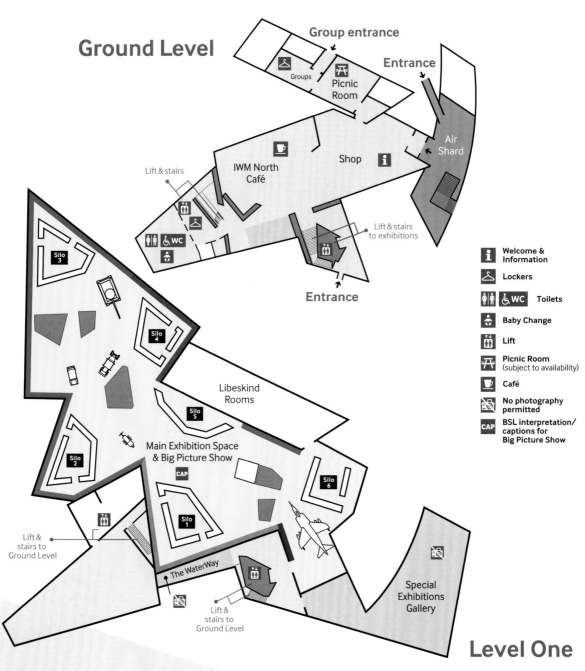

Group entrance

Groups

Picnic Room

Entrance

Air Shard

Lift & stairs

IWM North Café

Shop

Welcome & Information

Silo 3

WC

Lift & stairs to exhibitions

Entrance

Silo 4

Libeskind Rooms

Silo 5

Silo 2

Main Exhibition Space & Big Picture Show

CAP

Silo 6

Silo 1

Lift & stairs to Ground Level

The WaterWay

Lift & stairs to Ground Level

Special Exhibitions Gallery

Level One

i Welcome & Information

Lockers

WC Toilets

Baby Change

Lift

Picnic Room (subject to availability)

Café

No photography permitted

CAP BSL interpretation/ captions for Big Picture Show

Timeline

Introduction
1914 – 1918
1919 – 1938
1939 – 1945
1946 – 1990
1990 – Present

Silos

Silo 1 **Experience of War**

Silo 2 **Women & War**

Silo 3 **Impressions of War**

Silo 4 **Empire, Commonwealth & War**

Silo 5 **Science, Technology & War**

Silo 6 **Legacy of War**

CONTENTS

ABOUT YOUR GUIDEBOOK

Your guidebook follows the layout of the
Main Exhibition Space, moving from one
section of the exhibition's **Timeline** to the
next. It also covers each of the themed **Silo**
exhibitions in the order that they appear
along the route of the Timeline.

You can use it as a guide to your visit on the
day, and as a souvenir afterwards, when
you can enjoy the different perspective
that it gives to the exhibitions and displays.

For an explanation of how the Main
Exhibition Space works, see page 12.

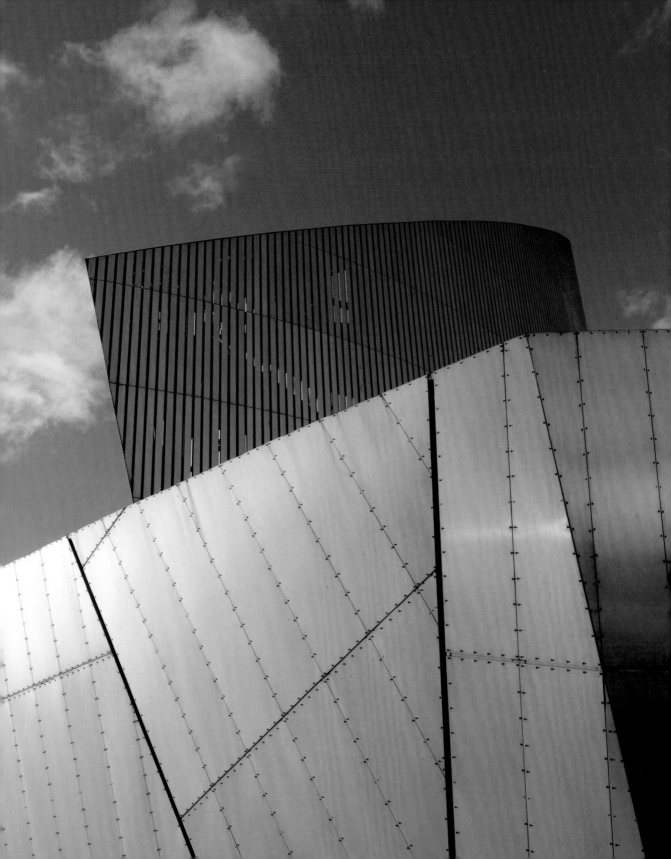

INTRODUCING IWM NORTH

When you visit IWM North, your experience begins long before you set foot inside the Main Exhibition Space. Instead it starts as soon as you catch sight of the iconic building in which the museum is housed — and the architecture continues to enrich your experience throughout your visit.

In the 1990s, IWM began looking for a location outside the south-east of England to build a new showcase for its unrivalled collections. Some 71 sites were offered to the museum but the wartime history of Trafford Park helped it to stand out.

It was here that dock workers unloaded vital supplies during the First and Second World Wars; here that factories churned out munitions, tanks, engines and radar systems; and here also that the Luftwaffe conducted many deadly bombing raids.

In 1997, world-renowned architect Daniel Libeskind was chosen to design the new museum. He had leapt to prominence in 1989 after winning the competition to design the Jewish Museum in Berlin. His insistence that the architecture of a museum should give richer meaning to its subject matter was just what IWM wanted.

DID YOU KNOW?

German bombers used the reflection of the moon in the water of Salford docks to help locate their target. In response, the authorities spread coal dust over the water to reduce its glare.

5

Trafford Park history
Female workers in a Trafford Park factory in 1918 prepare mattresses for use as boiler liners in battleships. The area was a key hub in the industrial effort required to keep Britain in the war.
IWM Q 28244

Leading the way (left)
Daniel Libeskind's award-winning IWM North building has been a catalyst for the regeneration of the entire Quays area.

DESIGN CHALLENGE

In its brief to the architects competing to build the new museum, IWM made several points clear. IWM North was not to be a 'military' museum, but one about the impact of war on individuals. It was to be a place of 'story-telling' – where visitors could find out what it feels like to be caught up in conflict. It was also to be an exhibit in itself – a building that people would want to see and experience for themselves.

It was just the kind of challenge to inspire an architect like Daniel Libeskind. He decided to place the destructive reality of war and its impact right at the very heart of his design.

DID YOU KNOW?
Daniel Libeskind sealed a spherical teapot in a plastic bag and dropped it out of the fourth floor window of his Berlin studio. He collected the fragments and used them as inspiration for the three shards you can see at IWM North.

THREE SHARDS

Libeskind imagined a globe torn apart by war and then set about constructing a building from three of its fragments — to represent conflict on land, in the air and on water. He deliberately arranged these fragments, which he called 'shards', in jagged, jarring confrontation to each other.

The **Earth Shard** houses the museum's Main Exhibition Space and Special Exhibition Gallery, its floor and roof curving downwards like the surface of the globe itself.

The **Air Shard** juts high into the skyline, announcing the presence of the museum below. The striking shape and height of the Air Shard adds a powerful silhouette to Manchester's ever-growing skyline.

The **Water Shard** undulates away from the rest of the museum, and houses our multi-purpose events spaces with captivating views over the waters of the Manchester Ship Canal.

Evolution of an idea (above)
Studio Daniel Libeskind produced this series of illustrations to show how the shards of IWM North represent a world fragmented by conflict.

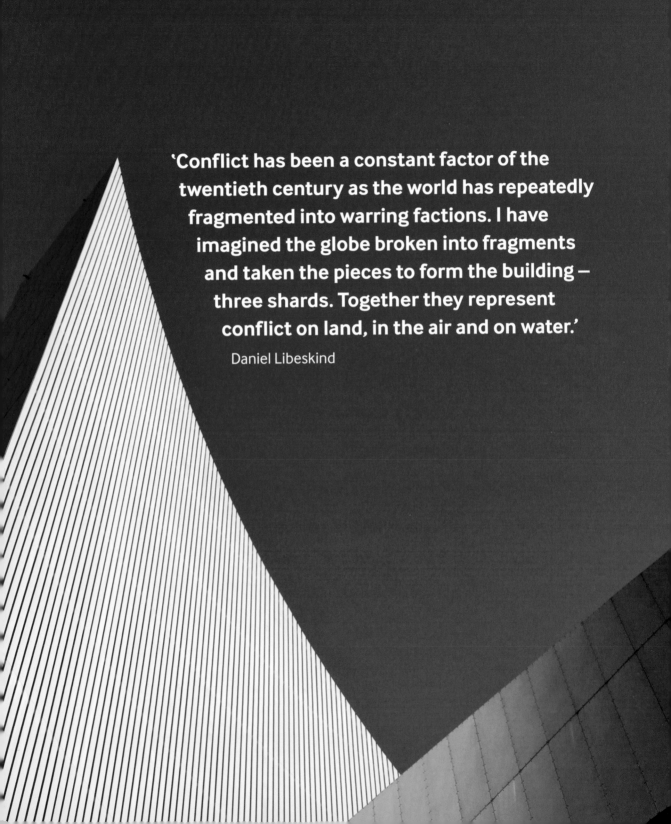

'Conflict has been a constant factor of the twentieth century as the world has repeatedly fragmented into warring factions. I have imagined the globe broken into fragments and taken the pieces to form the building — three shards. Together they represent conflict on land, in the air and on water.'

Daniel Libeskind

DANIEL LIBESKIND: ARCHITECT, VISIONARY, VIRTUOSO

Daniel Libeskind was born in Lodz, Poland in 1946, the second child of Polish Jewish parents who had survived the Holocaust. In 1959 his family emigrated to the USA, and in 1965 Daniel – by that time a virtuoso musician – became a United States citizen.

At around the same time, Daniel enrolled on a degree course in architecture, from which he graduated in 1970. He then embarked on a career in academia, teaching at institutions all over the world.

It was only in the late 1980s that he began to put theory into practice by setting up his own design studio in Berlin and winning the commission to build the Jewish Museum, which was completed in 1999.

In 2003, a year after IWM North was completed, Daniel was chosen to be the master planner for the redevelopment of the World Trade Center site in New York. His other projects include the Denver Art Museum in Colorado, USA, the Grand Canal Theatre in Dublin, Ireland, and the residential complex Reflections at Keppel Bay in Singapore.

© LEN GRANT

A BUILDING THAT ENRICHES YOUR VISIT

Every aspect of Daniel Libeskind's building – both inside and out – is intended to address the subject of war, giving you a physical experience to complement the emotion of the stories you will find in the exhibition spaces. Here are a few architectural details to look out for during your visit.

- As you enter IWM North at the foot of the Air Shard, you are still exposed to the elements in a space that isn't quite inside or outside. It is a deliberately strange environment.

- The Air Shard itself leans four degrees away from the vertical. This makes the rest of the world look out of kilter.

- Even the handrail on the staircase leading up to the exhibition spaces is not where you would expect it to be. It juts out at an odd angle to the wall, and the walls themselves feel like they are collapsing inwards.

- The floor of the Earth Shard is marked with the lines of latitude, linking it to the geographical reality of the globe itself. It also curves away in all directions from the entrance, creating a strangely disorientating effect. There is a remarkable drop of 8 feet from the entrance of the Main Exhibition Space to its far end.

- The recessed lighting in the Main Exhibition Space has been deliberately positioned to cut across the path of the Sun as it moves over the building. Visitors have likened the effect to tracer bullets and searchlights.

The Air Shard lights up to commemorate the 100th anniversary of the Battle of the Somme on Friday 1 July 2016 (right)
©PAUL HEYES

ESSENTIAL IWM NORTH

Every object on display at IWM North has the power to live on in your memory. It could be something big like the shelter used by fire watchers during the Blitz, or something small like the rubber bullets used to disperse rioters in Northern Ireland. But there are some exhibits and experiences that you simply must not miss.

REFLECT ON 9/11

Look out for the mangled steel section recovered from the ruins of the World Trade Center after the terror attacks of 11 September 2001. Watch and listen to eyewitness testimony from that shocking day and consider the words of poet Simon Armitage offered beneath the steel itself.

EXPERIENCE THE BIG PICTURE SHOWS

IWM North is famous for the award-winning 360° multimedia presentations that you can enjoy at regular intervals in the Main Exhibition Space. Listen out for the announcements and, as the lights dim, prepare for a powerful, immersive and thought-provoking experience. For more on the Big Picture Shows, see page 14.

DISCOVER OUR ART

IWM North commissions artists to create their own responses to the subject of war. Look out for examples throughout your visit, such as the Crusader sculpture by Gerry Judah just inside the entrance to the Main Exhibition Space.

ICONIC LARGE OBJECTS

Discover our iconic large objects throughout the Main Exhibition Space, beginning with our US Harrier suspended above the entrance. Delve further into the exhibition space to discover more of our impressive collection, including the Field Gun which fired the first shot for the British Army in the First World War.

CATCH THE LATEST SPECIAL EXHIBITIONS

Make sure you take a look at the Special Exhibitions Gallery to see the latest in our changing programme of often award-winning displays. Look out also for separate displays throughout the museum — especially in the WaterWay.

AND DON'T MISS

- The **pistol** carried during the First World War by **JRR Tolkien**, author of *The Hobbit* and *The Lord of the Rings*.

- The ingeniously constructed **compass** used by Oliver Philpot during a successful escape from a Second World War prisoner of war camp.

- The set of **Iraqi Most Wanted playing cards** issued to US soldiers before the Iraq War in 2003.

MAIN EXHIBITION SPACE

There are many ways to experience the **Main Exhibition Space** within the Earth Shard. You can follow the story of war year by year, or explore particular themes. You can listen to people talking about their experiences of conflict, or examine objects of war with your own hands.

'Your idea of what a museum should be like will be blown away.'

Janet Street-Porter

FOLLOW THE TIMELINE

Running around the walls of the Main Exhibition Space is a **Timeline** that guides you through the key events of twentieth and twenty-first century warfare. It tells you the story of war, introducing important personalities, presenting thought-provoking facts and figures, and providing a context for individual decisions, offensives, victories and defeats. It also brings you the sight, sound, touch and feel of war – via a wealth of objects, films, audio recordings and hands-on interactive displays known as **Action Stations**.

The Timeline starts on your left-hand side as you enter the Main Exhibition Space. It is split into five parts, each of which is covered in your guidebook.

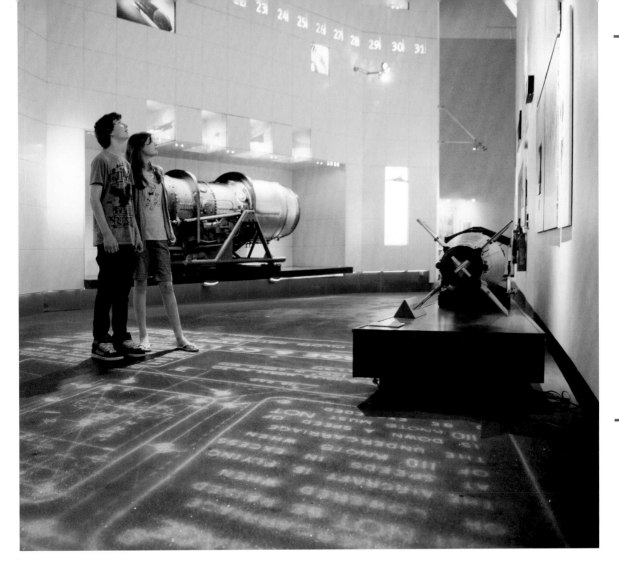

EXPLORE THE SILOS

As you follow the Timeline around the walls of the Main Exhibition Space, you will pass six towering spaces that we call **Silos**. Each Silo is a mini-exhibition focusing on a different theme – a theme common to all wars from 1914 to the present day.

Each Silo approaches its subject in a different way, offering you an interesting change of tone and atmosphere, and giving an alternative impact to the objects and stories that they contain.

You can find out more about the Silos throughout the guidebook.

MEET OUR VOLUNTEERS

Look out for our object handling sessions where our volunteers (subject to availability) will help you get closer to the artefacts and explain the amazing stories behind them. On certain days, there is a very special chance to meet veterans and eyewitnesses, to hear their personal stories of conflict and ask questions with your family.

EXPERIENCE THE BIG PICTURE SHOW

At least once every hour, the lights dim in the Main Exhibition Space and the scene is set for one of our award-winning **Big Picture Shows**. Images play across the walls all around you. Voices, sounds and music fill the air. It is an enveloping and often moving experience that captures the consuming power of war, raises difficult questions, and provokes discussion and debate.

The daily schedule of the shows can vary. You can find the latest schedule online at **iwm.org.uk**, or listen out for announcements during the day.

REMEMBRANCE
Discover the different ways in which we remember conflict from the First World War through to Iraq.

AL MUTANABBI STREET: A REACTION
Witness a creative response to a bomb attack on Baghdad's busy Al-Mutanabbi Street

THE WAR AT HOME
Ordinary men and women explain what life was like on the home front during the Second World War.

CHILDREN AND WAR
Boys and girls discuss what it is like to be caught up in war — as evacuees, refugees, targets and combatants.

MIGHTIER THAN WAR
This is a creative response by poet Tony Walsh, exploring the 'human spirit' during conflict.

LIFE ON THE LINE
Footage from acclaimed film director Peter Jackson's *They Shall Not Grow Old* features digitally transformed film, photographs and audio from IWM's First World War collection.

Please be aware that when the Big Picture Show is on, the exhibition space will go dark and there will be loud noises and flashing images which some visitors may find unsettling.

FIRST WORLD WAR 1914 – 1918

The first section of the Timeline in the Main Exhibition Space covers the shattering events of 1914 to 1918, explaining how the First World War swept across Europe and beyond. It begins by looking at the troubled summer of 1914 and the reasons why the world went to war.

The delicate balance of power between Europe's leading nations was disturbed by the dramatic rise of Germany following its unification in 1871. Russia and France formed an alliance, pushing Germany closer to its own ally Austria-Hungary. Britain had understandings with France and Russia but was not formally allied to either.

The assassination of Archduke Franz Ferdinand — heir to the Austro-Hungarian throne — by a Serbian-backed terrorist raised tensions between allies on both sides. Austria-Hungary declared war on Serbia, hostilities escalated, and on 4 August 1914 Britain came in on the side of Russia and France.

Portrait of war
Mud by Gilbert Rogers, 1919.
The painting, which captures the misery of life at the front, is on display in the Main Exhibition Space.
IWM ART 3734

DID YOU KNOW?
The First World War was a truly global conflict. The first British shot was fired in Togoland on 12 August 1914 by Sergeant Major Alhaji Grunshi of the Gold Coast Regiment.

'Come along boys and join the army... our cheery lads need your help.'

Recruiting poster, November 1914

FIRST WORLD WAR TIMELINE
When war broke out in 1914, neither side expected it to go on for four long years. The timeline shown here is an edited version of the one in the exhibition. It details the main events of the war — the quick descent into deadlock, the attempts to break it, and the eventual and sudden end.

28 JULY 1914
A month after the heir to the Austro-Hungarian throne is assassinated by a Bosnian terrorist, Austria-Hungary declares war on Serbia

4 AUGUST 1914
After agonising over whether to support its friend France, Britain declares war on Germany when the latter invades neutral Belgium

1914–1917
THE WESTERN FRONT

Both sides quickly discovered that this war was going to be like no other. The power and accuracy of modern artillery fire drove soldiers to dig into the ground simply to survive. By the end of December 1914, a network of trenches had evolved, running from the Belgian coast to Switzerland.

The British, French and Germans launched huge offensives in an attempt to break through these defences — notably at Ypres in 1915, Verdun and the Somme in 1916, and Passchendaele in 1917. All came at a terrible cost and none were decisive.

DID YOU KNOW?

Many sports competitions were suspended during the First World War. The last FA Cup Final of the war was played at Old Trafford on 24 April 1915. Sheffield Wednesday beat Chelsea 3—0.

A life of dreary discomfort
The biscuits issued to British soldiers were not popular. The message written on this example reads: 'Your King and country need you and this is how they feed you'.
IWM EPH 1338

Shell shock
Artillery proved to be the key weapon in the First World War. However, it wasn't until 1917 that Britain had enough heavy guns and shells to provide the kind of concentrated fire required to break through enemy lines. This 4.5-inch shrapnel shell was designed to target enemy infantry. It contained almost 500 metal balls, which would shoot out in all directions when the shell exploded.
IWM MUN 661

AUGUST–SEPTEMBER 1914	OCTOBER 1914	DECEMBER 1914	FEBRUARY 1915
Germany crushes a Russian advance in East Prussia. In the west, Allied troops halt the Germans at the Battle of the Marne, close to Paris.	Turkey joins with Germany and Austria-Hungary against the Allies	Two opposing lines of trenches stretch from the Belgian coast to Switzerland, forming the Western Front	The Allies launch a naval assault on Turkey. Troops are later landed at Gallipoli, but the campaign ends in failure in 1916.

1914–1918
THE WAR IN THE AIR

For the first time in any war, the skies became part of the battlefield. Both sides quickly began to use aircraft to fly over enemy trenches, observing troop movements, spotting potential targets and directing artillery fire.

Fighter planes equipped with guns and bombs were developed to counter enemy aircraft and attack ground troops. Mid-air duels became common, with the British Royal Flying Corps at first suffering heavy losses to superior German machines. It was only in 1917, with the arrival of a new generation of fighter planes like the Sopwith Camel, that the balance in air power began to tip decisively in favour of Britain.

High flier
The Royal Flying Corps tunic worn by highly decorated fighter pilot Captain Albert Ball, VC (see below).
IWM UNI 11617

CAPTAIN ALBERT BALL, VC: FIGHTER PILOT, AIR ACE, CELEBRITY

Captain Albert Ball was one of the most famous of the First World War flying 'aces' – the name given to any airman credited with shooting down more than five enemy planes. By April 1917, Albert had accounted for 44 such victories, earning himself the Distinguished Service Order and the Military Cross.

Albert had just turned eighteen when he joined the Army in September 1914. He learned to fly in 1915, transferred to the Royal Flying Corps the following year and then joined a fighter unit in May 1916. Between May and October in that year alone, he recorded 30 victories and reluctantly found himself fêted in the national press. On 7 May 1917, after engaging enemy aircraft 26 times in less than two weeks, he failed to return from a patrol over northern France. He was just twenty years old.

Ace among aces
Captain Albert Ball was awarded a posthumous Victoria Cross in June 1917 for 'conspicuous and consistent bravery'.   IWM Q 68085

MAY 1915
Hoping to knock Russia out of the war, Germany begins a series of successful offensives in the east. But Russia proves too strong to defeat in a single campaign.

21 FEBRUARY 1916
The Germans attack the fortress of Verdun, hoping to force France out of the war. But the French Army holds firm.

31 MAY 1916
The British and German fleets clash in the Battle of Jutland (left). The battle is indecisive but the Germans do not venture out again.
IWM SP 2156

BEYOND THE WESTERN FRONT

With the Western Front in deadlock, both sides searched further afield for ways to win the war. In Eastern Europe and the Balkans, Britain and France looked to their ally Russia to take the fight to Germany and Austria-Hungary.

In October 1914, Turkey came in against Russia, plunging the Caucasus into war, and forcing British and Empire troops to mount a defence of Mesopotamia, Egypt and Palestine.

With clashes in Africa and the Pacific, this was truly a world war, placing terrific strain on the armies and economies of the combatant nations. It proved to be a strain under which the great empires of Russia, Austria-Hungary and Turkey would break apart.

DID YOU KNOW?

In April 1915 King George V announced that he would abstain from alcohol for the duration of the war; no wine, beer or spirits were served in royal residences until 11 November 1918, when an 1815 cognac was opened by Royal Command.

Wider war

A field cap worn by the 5th Royal Hungarian Honved Hussar regiment. Austro-Hungarian troops fought on the Western Front, in Italy, in the east and in the Middle East.

IWM UNI 9259

1914 – 1918 THE WAR AT SEA

Before the war, Germany spent enormous sums building a fleet to rival Britain's Royal Navy. In the end, the two fleets clashed directly only once – at the Battle of Jutland in May 1916 – and the result was inconclusive.

Both sides chose instead to mount blockades to starve each other of food and raw materials. From August 1914, the Royal Navy patrolled the Channel and North Sea, turning away ships heading for Germany and seizing their cargoes. In February 1915, the Germans retaliated by mounting submarine attacks without warning on ships heading for Britain.

The Germans scaled back this campaign for fear that it would provoke America to enter the war against them. However, they gambled on a renewal of the campaign in February 1917 as an alternative to the costly land battles of the previous year. It backfired. On 6 April 1917, America joined the war.

1 JULY 1916	1 FEBRUARY 1917	MARCH 1917	6 APRIL 1917
Allied troops attack on the Somme – the most costly day of the war for the British Army. A bitter struggle continues into November.	German submarines begin to attack without warning all ships sailing to Allied ports, aiming to starve Britain out of the war within six months	Tsar Nicholas II is forced to abdicate as revolution breaks out in Russia. By the year's end the communist Bolshevik Party has seized power.	The USA enters the war, provoked by German attacks on its shipping and a German attempt to gain Mexico as an ally in the event of war with the USA

ADA RODGERS: WORKER, MUNITIONETTE, GANGER

Women had always formed a significant part of Britain's working population, but during the First World War they began to take on jobs previously reserved for men. In the year from June 1915, some 563,000 women began working in war industries, attempting to meet the Army's increasing demand for shells, ammunition, weapons and other supplies. Ada Rodgers was one such worker, operating machinery and leading a 'gang' of other women at a munitions factory in Sheffield from March 1916 to December 1918. Women like Ada were known as 'munitionettes' and some became known as 'canaries', their skin and hair dyed yellow by the dangerous chemicals that they had to handle.

War worker
This photograph of Ada Rodgers in her overalls is displayed in the Timeline alongside a certificate recognising her years of war industry service.
IWM DOCUMENTS.10721

1914 – 1918
HOME FRONT

As the demands from the fighting front grew, the lives of British civilians became ever more subject to government interference. A Ministry of Munitions was set up in 1915 to manage war production, opening huge factories filled with workers not needed by the Army – the old, the very young and women.

A shortfall in Army recruitment saw the introduction of conscription in early 1916, and the German blockade on shipping led to such severe food shortages that rationing was introduced in 1918.

Meanwhile, from 1915 onwards, civilians across the country found themselves targeted by bombing raids from Zeppelin airships and other aircraft. This was a war fought too close to home for comfort.

POLICE NOTICE
ALL CLEAR

Danger from above
Police cyclists carried this cardboard notice with them to signal the end of a German air raid. During the course of the war, some 1,413 British men, women and children died as a result of enemy bombs.
IWM FEQ 177

APRIL 1917	JULY 1917	9 DECEMBER 1917	3 MARCH 1918
A failed French offensive triggers a series of mutinies that seriously weaken the French Army for the rest of the year	A British assault begins at Ypres but is hindered by rain and mud. The attack ends after the capture of Passchendaele in November.	Jerusalem surrenders to British and Empire forces during a successful campaign against Turkey in Palestine	Germany and the other Central Powers sign the Treaty of Brest-Litovsk with communist Russia ending the war on the Eastern Front

1918
THE WESTERN FRONT

In autumn 1917, a breakdown in food supplies sparked a revolution in Russia, eventually forcing the country's withdrawal from the war. Germany could now transfer more men to the Western Front and push for all-out victory before American troops arrived to reinforce the British and French.

The German offensive came in March 1918 and the Allied lines were breached. A much more mobile war followed in which the Allies retreated and regrouped, before launching an effective counter-attack of their own in August. With the US Army soon lending its weight, the Allies made a further breakthrough at the beginning of October. The German Army began to crack, revolution threatened at home and the Kaiser was forced to abdicate. The end came on 11 November 1918 with the signing of the Armistice. The war was over.

DID YOU KNOW?
Kaiser Wilhelm II abdicated on 9 November 1918 and fled to neutral Holland where he remained in exile until his death on 4 June 1941. On arrival he surprised his Dutch host by asking for 'a nice cup of English tea'.

Advances in technology
Much of the weaponry and technology used by soldiers in 1918 was not available at the beginning of the war. This German sub-machine gun, which gave its infantry invaluable automatic firepower, was only issued months before the end of the war. It was captured during a British attack on 17 October 1918.
IWM FIR 6091

Peace at last (right)
Officers of the 1st Battalion, Irish Guards, read details of the Armistice with Germany to their men at Maubeuge in France, November 1918.
IWM Q 3365

21 MARCH 1918
Germany launches a Spring Offensive (right). Weathering the storm, the Allies counter successfully from July.
IWM Q 55020

SEPTEMBER 1918
British Empire forces rout the Turkish Army in Palestine. The surrender of Bulgaria exposes Constantinople to attack. Defeat looms for Turkey.

NOVEMBER 1918
Defeats force Germany to request an armistice, on 4 October 1918. But the fighting continues until the armistice agreement is signed on 11 November.

EXPERIENCE OF WAR

What is it like to live in a world at war? To volunteer to join the army? To be a soldier taken prisoner, or a civilian marched off to an internment camp? To be a child evacuated from your home or even your country, separated, perhaps permanently, from your family? These are some of the experiences of war explored in this Silo — stories of ordinary men, women and children from 1914 through to the present day who have lived and died amid the tumult of war.

24

'We are all amazed that we are still alive let alone still working'

Frederick Thompson, British prisoner of war forced to work in Japan, 1942 – 1945

Art of survival

Tens of thousands of German and Turkish servicemen were captured during the First World War and sent to prison camps. They only returned home in 1920 once formal peace treaties had been ratified. This snake was made from glass beads by Turkish prisoners sometime between 1918 and 1919.

IWM EPH 2489

Love and war

To boost the number of recruits to the Army during the First World War, men from the same community, workplace or social club were encouraged to form their own battalions – popularly known as Pals battalions. This sweetheart's brooch was made from the cap badge of the Liverpool Pals.

IWM INS 6139

Leaving home behind

In the months leading up to the Second World War, around 10,000 Jewish children were sent to Britain by parents desperate to protect them from the growing Nazi menace. One of these children was Arnold Urbach, who carried this suitcase with him on his journey from Germany.

IWM EPH 2471

Marking time

Sam Hughes was a corporal serving with No. 84 Squadron, Royal Air Force when he was taken prisoner by the Japanese in Java in March 1942. He was issued with this aluminium mess bowl, which he proceeded to decorate with the badge of his squadron, the date of his capture and the date of his eventual release in August 1945.

IWM EPH 385

LOOK OUT FOR...

- The camp magazine created by British internees at Ruhleben in Germany in 1916. It was bound with the skin of rats killed in the camp.

- The typewriter grabbed by a British journalist moments after being chased from his bath by Japanese troops during the fall of Singapore in 1942. He was captured carrying the typewriter and wearing only a pith helmet.

- An apron from the Second World War, sewn by an inmate in a Japanese civilian internment camp in Sumatra, Indonesia. The apron was a gift for Miss Margaret Dryburgh, who later died in this camp.

BETWEEN THE WARS 1919–1939

The second section of the Timeline covers the twenty year period between the end of the First World War and the beginning of the Second. It charts the attempts to preserve the hard-won peace, the rise of extreme political movements and the rebirth of Germany as a military power.

In 1919 the victorious Allies met in Paris to agree a peace settlement, resulting in a treaty signed at the Palace of Versailles on 28 June. Under its terms, Germany was stripped of arms and territory, and ordered to pay stringent financial reparations.

The Allies also agreed to form the League of Nations — a new international body designed to settle disputes without the need for war. It would prove to be a difficult task amid the political and economic instability of the years ahead.

Building the peace
US President Woodrow Wilson signs the Peace Treaty in the Hall of Mirrors at Versailles in June 1919. The treaty would help to shape the events of the next two decades.
IWM Q 14997

> *'This is not peace. It is an armistice for twenty years.'*
>
> *Marshal Foch, French Army, 28 June 1919*

DID YOU KNOW?
In 1923, some 4,000 headstones were still being delivered each week to cemeteries in France to replace the wooden crosses originally used to mark the final resting place of the British and Empire dead.

BETWEEN THE WARS TIMELINE
The political, economic and military landscape of Europe changed enormously in the 1920s and 1930s, while growing tension in Asia erupted into war between China and Japan. The key events of these troubled decades are covered here.

28 JUNE 1919
A peace treaty between Germany and the Allies is signed at the Palace of Versailles, near Paris

1925
The Locarno Treaty reconciles Germany with her former enemies. Three years later, 15 nations sign the Kellogg-Briand Pact which seeks to ban war.

SAFE FOR DEMOCRACY

The League of Nations was the brainchild of US President Woodrow Wilson, who hoped that it would help to create a world 'safe for democracy'. Yet, when the new organisation met for the first time in London in 1920, the US had already withdrawn from participation, its government determined to isolate itself from the problems of Europe.

Fighting continued in many regions throughout the 1920s – most notably in Russia where a civil war claimed the lives of millions. Britain too was beset with troubles. Towards the end of the First World War, nationalists in Ireland had embarked on a campaign of guerrilla warfare. Eventually, in 1921, the British government agreed to divide Ireland into a southern Free State and a British-ruled Northern Ireland, but fighting would continue in the South for a further two years.

The terms of the peace in 1919 also saw the creation of new nations from the ruins of the Austro-Hungarian, Turkish and Russian Empires. The imposition of new borders and governments brought new rivalries, new ethnic minorities and the rise of extreme political movements to the left and right.

Far from being safe for democracy, many parts of Europe became dominated by dictatorships – from the communist Stalin in Russia to the fascist Mussolini in Italy. Tensions were set to rise still further in the 1930s, as the world fell into the grip of an economic depression.

DID YOU KNOW?

Benito Mussolini, the fascist leader of Italy from 1922 to 1943, was initially admired by the world's democracies. In 1923 he was awarded an honorary knighthood by King George V.

Revolution remembered

A plate made in 1923 to commemorate the achievements of the Red Army in Russia. It depicts one of its soldiers standing over symbols of the Tsar that the Army helped to depose.
IWM EPH 3397

24 OCTOBER 1929	SEPTEMBER 1931	30 JANUARY 1933	SEPTEMBER 1935
A panic begins on Wall Street, America's financial centre. It sparks the Great Depression, bringing economic and political chaos to the early 1930s.	In defiance of the League of Nations, Japanese troops invade the Chinese province of Manchuria	Adolf Hitler, head of the Nazi Party, becomes Germany's leader, establishing a dictatorship based on mass persuasion, coercion, violence and terror	The 'Nuremberg Laws' make German Jews outcasts. Jews lose their citizenship, and are forbidden to marry or have sex with non-Jews.

Fascism in Britain

A badge worn by members of the British Union of Fascists, a movement established in 1932 by politician Oswald Mosley.

IWM INS 3669

Military dictatorship

Members of the Italian Fascist Militia wore round black caps like this. The fascist movement in Italy was led by Benito Mussolini, who held power for 21 years.

IWM UNI 8226

THOMAS FANNING: COMMUNIST, FIGHTER, AMPUTEE

Among the exhibits in this section of the Timeline are a book and a certificate of repatriation belonging to Manchester man Thomas Fanning. An active member of the Labour Party and Communist Party since the mid-1920s, Thomas volunteered to join the International Brigade in 1936 to fight against right-wing Nationalist forces in the Spanish Civil War. He was one of tens of thousands of young men to do the same from all around the world.

In February 1937, Thomas was wounded at the Battle of Jarama and lost one of his legs. The war itself ended in 1939 when the Nationalists claimed victory thanks in part to heavy support from Germany and Italy.

United by politics

A group of International Brigade men in 1937. That same year their comrade Thomas Fanning was invalided back to Britain.

IWM HU 34656

2 OCTOBER 1935

Italy invades Abyssinia – now Ethiopia. The capital falls in May 1936 and Mussolini (right) hails Italy's new empire.

IWM FLM 1506

7 MARCH 1936

German troops re-occupy the Rhineland. Despite this violation of the Treaty of Versailles, Britain and France take no action.

JULY 1936

The Spanish Civil War begins when right-wing generals revolt against the government. Nearly 500,000 die before the end of the war in 1939.

GERMANY BETWEEN THE WARS

The First World War ended in revolution for Germany. The Kaiser was forced to abdicate and a new form of democratic government – the Weimar Republic – was put in place. But Germany itself remained an outcast within Europe. Its economy was so crippled that it soon defaulted on the massive financial reparations demanded by the Treaty of Versailles, and in 1923 it had to watch as French and Belgian troops occupied its industrial heartland to ensure that it didn't happen again.

By 1929, the German economy had stabilised but was nowhere near strong enough to withstand the effects of the Great Depression. Millions lost their jobs and looked to the radical Nazi party – and its charismatic leader Adolf Hitler – for a solution.

The Nazis were swept into office in 1933 and quickly tore up the hated Treaty of Versailles. Democracy descended into dictatorship, as Hitler eliminated his political opponents and began a campaign of persecution against what he termed 'alien' influences, including Jews, 'Gypsies' (Roma and Sinti), Jehovah's Witnesses, homosexuals, the disabled and the mentally ill.

The Nazis were determined to restore what Germany had lost in the First World War – its military pride and economic might – but they also wanted to go further, seizing territory in the Rhineland, Austria and Czechoslovakia.

Each step of the way, the leaders of Britain and France gave in to Hitler's demands, hoping somehow to avoid a new war. At the Munich Conference in September 1938, Prime Minister Neville Chamberlain claimed that he had secured 'peace for our time' – by convincing Hitler to pursue diplomatic rather than military solutions. Hitler, however, told his ministers not to take the agreement seriously and in 1939 began making claims on territory in Poland.

The time for appeasement had passed. Both sides looked to form alliances and stepped up preparations for a war that appeared to grow more and more inevitable with each passing day.

30

Toys in uniform

These dolls were bought in Germany in 1931. The one on the left shows a member of the *Schutzstaffel* (SS), the other the *Sturmabteilung* (SA) – both Nazi paramilitary groups. Hitler is said to have frowned upon the dolls as looking too effeminate.

IWM EPH 2482, 2483

JULY 1937

Fighting breaks out again between China and Japan – the start of a conflict that lasts until 1945, engulfing the whole of Asia

MARCH 1938

Hitler annexes Austria (right). He then demands the German-speaking part of Czechoslovakia.

IWM NYP 68062

SEPTEMBER 1938

At the Munich Conference, the British and French give in to Hitler's demands. Tearing up the Munich Agreement, Hitler occupies the rest of Czechoslovakia in March 1939.

Ascent to power
Adolf Hitler climbs to the speaker's podium
during the 1934 Harvest Thanksgiving Ceremony
at Bückeberg. His aggressive policies would lead
to war before the end of the decade.
IWM MH 11040

APRIL 1939
Poland appears to be
Hitler's next victim. Britain
and France guarantee her
independence.

MAY 1939
Germany and Italy
conclude a military
and diplomatic alliance

23 AUGUST 1939
Hitler signs a non-
aggression pact with
Russia. Its secret clauses
allow for a German
invasion of Poland.

**1 SEPTEMBER
1939**
Germany invades
Poland. Two days later
Europe is at war again.

WOMEN AND WAR

As Britain's men joined the armed forces during the First and Second World Wars, women began to fill their places. Some worked in fields or factories, others as nurses or journalists. Many chose to join the armed forces themselves, serving as cooks and drivers, operating barrage balloons and anti-aircraft batteries, and some even worked undercover behind enemy lines. Their experiences — recorded in this Silo — document a wider shift in the role of women in society.

Tried for treason

A cloth tag taken from the door of the cell that held British nurse Edith Cavell in the weeks leading up to her execution by a German firing squad in October 1915. The 49-year-old Cavell had helped some 200 Allied soldiers escape from occupied Belgium.

IWM EPH 3158

Military trailblazer

This Echeverria 7.65mm pistol was carried by Flora Sandes (right), the only British woman to fight as a soldier in the First World War. Sandes fought in the Serbian army and was seriously wounded in 1916.

IWM FIR 3253, Q 32702

Campaigning for peace

Women have often been at the forefront of anti-war movements. In September 1981, a group of women established a 'peace camp' outside RAF Greenham Common to protest against the decision to site 96 American cruise missiles at the base. One of the women produced badges like this one to help raise money for the protest.

IWM EPH 3264

Undercover agent

Yvonne Cormeau was a radio operator with the Special Operations Executive during the Second World War. Codenamed 'Annette', she was parachuted into occupied France and spent 13 months masquerading as a district nurse, while secretly arranging drops of weapons and other supplies for use by the French Resistance. A dress worn by Cormeau can be seen in the displays.

IWM HU 47367

> ## 'We had two half pints of milk a day to keep out the poison.'
>
> *Elsie McIntyre, First World War munitions worker*

Aid worker

Emma Kay carried this ID card while working for the International Medical Corps in Kosovo. It was her job to help set up mobile clinics to deal with the humanitarian crisis triggered by war in the region.

IWM EPH 3013

LOOK OUT FOR...

- The uniform worn by singer and movie star Marlene Dietrich while entertaining the troops in Europe during the Second World War.

- The George Medal awarded to 15-year-old Charity Bick for her bravery as a despatch rider in West Bromwich during Nazi air raids.

- The reporter's notebook used by Kate Adie during her time as a war correspondent in the former Yugoslavia.

Headline news
A newspaper seller carries a placard announcing that Britain has declared war on Germany.
IWM HU 36171

SECOND WORLD WAR 1939–1945

The events of 1939 to 1945 are covered in the third section of the Timeline. It shows how campaigns were fought back and forth across continents and oceans, killing some 55 million people and leaving millions more homeless — a global conflict with a global impact.

After the outbreak of war, British troops began taking up positions behind the Allied lines near the Belgian border. But for seven months, there was no significant action on the Western Front, and the British press began to talk about the conflict as a 'Phoney War'.

Then on 10 May 1940 came a lightning-quick German offensive. Troops thundered their way through Allied lines and conquered Luxembourg, Holland and France within weeks. By June 1940, Britain was alone, at bay and fearing invasion. The future looked bleak.

'Close your hearts to pity, act brutally.'

Adolf Hitler, 22 August 1939

DID YOU KNOW?

Between September 1939 and January 1940 over 2.5 million British children and others were evacuated to areas thought safe from German bombing raids.

SECOND WORLD WAR TIMELINE

Fighting in the Second World War ranged far and wide, from the Arctic to the Pacific, north-west Europe to the Soviet Union, North Africa to the Far East. It lasted almost six years, claiming the lives of over 55 million men, women and children.

3 SEPTEMBER 1939

Two days after the Germans invade Poland, Britain, France, Australia and New Zealand all declare war on Germany

9 APRIL 1940

Germany invades Norway to prevent the Allies from cutting off its vital supply of iron ore from Sweden. They march into Denmark the same day.

WAR AT SEA

The war at sea was fought from the first day of the Second World War until the last – starting in the Atlantic and spreading south and east into the Mediterranean and Pacific.

For Britain and Germany, it was a battle for supply lines – defending their own and cutting off those of the enemy. As soon as war was declared, Royal Navy ships closed off the seas around Germany, and in response the Germans used U-boats to target British shipping.

This 'U-boat peril' was the one thing that really scared Prime Minister Winston Churchill during the war. He knew it could leave Britain incapable of sustaining its military efforts. It was only when British codebreakers managed to decipher Germany's U-boat signals that the tide began to turn. From the summer of 1943, the Royal Navy was able to find the right combination of intelligence,

technology and tactics to provide adequate protection for their convoys of merchant ships.

In the Pacific, Japan entered the war in December 1941 with an attack on the US naval base at Pearl Harbor. The Japanese enjoyed a few months of sustained success, until the US Navy secured a decisive victory at the Battle of Midway in June 1942. It was a naval battle of a kind never seen before. No ship ever came within firing distance of the enemy. Instead each side attacked with aircraft launched from carriers.

From that point on, US forces were able to advance island by island across the Pacific until they could establish air bases within striking distance of Japan. Then came the bombing raids that culminated in August 1945 with the dropping of atomic bombs on Hiroshima and Nagasaki.

WILLIAM CRAWFORD: LOVING SON, BOY SEAMAN, CASUALTY

Boy of war
William Crawford trained on HMS *Caledonia* before transferring to HMS *Belfast* in 1939.
IWM HU 64385

Among the objects on display in this section of the Timeline are a letter, diary, card and photograph belonging to William Macfarlane Crawford. Known as 'Bill' to his friends, William was born in Scotland on 13 July 1923 and was a sixteen-year-old Boy Seaman in the Royal Navy by the time war broke out in 1939. He spent the opening weeks of the war on HMS *Belfast*, helping to enforce the blockade on ships heading towards Germany.

When *Belfast* was damaged by a mine in November 1939, William was transferred to the battle cruiser HMS *Hood* along with some of his fellow Boy Seamen. In May 1941, HMS *Hood* was ordered to intercept the German battleship *Bismarck* and the heavy cruiser *Prinz Eugen*. She engaged the enemy on 24 May 1941 in the Battle of Denmark Strait, but was struck by several German shells. An explosion then ripped through the ship and *Hood* was sunk with the loss of all but three of her 1,418-strong crew. At seventeen years and ten months old, Bill Crawford is believed to have been the youngest member of the crew killed.

10 MAY 1940
Hitler launches a devastating offensive in the west. Six weeks later the French are forced to surrender.

4 JUNE 1940
The evacuation from Dunkirk ends. Some 250,000 British troops are rescued (right), allowing Britain to keep fighting.
IWM H 1623

10 JUNE 1940
Italy enters the war on Germany's side and in September invades Egypt from Libya

DID YOU KNOW?

British soldiers were issued with Benzedrine — an amphetamine taken to counteract battle fatigue. James Bond uses the same stimulant in several of Ian Fleming's novels.

Prepared for trouble

A first aid kit from 1940 containing shell dressings, bandages, tourniquets and zinc-oxide plaster.

IWM SUR 542

LAND WAR IN EUROPE

The German offensive in May 1940 ended with the British Army scrambling on to a hastily assembled fleet of ships and small boats at the French port of Dunkirk. Preparations soon began for an invasion of the continental mainland, but it would take years before they came to fruition.

In the meantime, German troops conquered Yugoslavia, Greece and Crete in April and May 1941, and launched an invasion of Russia the following month. Britain hit back at Germany at sea, from the air and in the deserts of North Africa, but had to wait until June 1944 before launching a direct assault on the ground in north-west Europe.

On 6 June 1944 — D-Day — an armada of ships crossed the English Channel carrying a huge force

of British, Canadian and American troops and equipment. By nightfall, supported by fighter planes and bombers, they had a firm foothold along a 50-mile stretch of the French coastline.

In the east, Russia had held firm against German offensives in the summers of 1941 and 1942, and then began advancing themselves in the summer of 1943. By autumn 1944, they were fighting on German territory.

Several months of fierce fighting followed on both fronts — and up through Italy from September 1943. In March 1945, Allied troops crossed the Rhine to begin their main assault on Germany, and Berlin finally surrendered to the Russians at the beginning of May. Days later the land war in Europe was over.

JULY 1940	SEPTEMBER 1940	FEBRUARY 1941	22 JUNE 1941
The Battle of Britain begins, as the Luftwaffe vies unsuccessfully with the Royal Air Force for control of the skies over southern England	Germany subjects Britain to the 'Blitz' — nine months of bombing raids on cities and towns designed to force Britain to surrender	German troops arrive in North Africa to reinforce the Italians, who have been forced back into Libya by British troops	After conquering Yugoslavia, Greece and Crete in April and May, Germany launches a full-scale invasion of the Soviet Union

WAR EFFORT

The burden of the war effort was shared across an unprecedented proportion of the British public. From 1941, women were conscripted to enter the armed forces or work in war industries. By June 1944 a third of the population was engaged in war work.

Many people volunteered to work in the evenings or at the weekends on top of their day jobs. Some joined the Home Guard or the Special Constabulary. Others became Civil Defence wardens or members of the Fire Guard. Uniforms, helmets, armbands and badges — sporting a bewildering array of acronyms — became a commonplace sight on the streets.

Those not involved in war work could not escape the effects of war. The threat of air raids meant that many homes were fitted with bomb shelters, and strict rationing made every meal a reminder of the ongoing conflict. The whole of Britain was at war.

DID YOU KNOW?
Wartime bride Helen Landsell made herself some wedding day earrings from the windscreen of a crashed German aircraft. The star-shaped glass earrings are on display in the Timeline cabinets.

Wider war

Some 250,000 men not eligible for the regular Army joined the Local Defence Volunteers (renamed the Home Guard in July 1940) in its first 24 hours. Since most of its members were too old for conscription, the organisation was nicknamed 'Dad's Army'.

IWM INS 3780

AIR ATTACK

After the withdrawal of the British Army at Dunkirk, the only way to take the fight directly to Germany was from the air — and the best chance of success lay in night-time bombing raids.

RAF bomber crews had to brave a wall of fire to reach enemy territory — running a gauntlet of searchlights, radar, night fighters and anti-aircraft guns that stretched from Paris to Denmark. To begin with, their planes didn't have the range to penetrate deep into Germany, and they could not drop their bombs with enough accuracy to inflict the right kind of strategic damage.

In 1942, longer range heavy bombers like the Lancaster and Halifax came into service. There was also a switch from targeted raids to so-called area bombing, in which waves of bombers would subject German cities and industrial regions to concentrated — and later controversial — attack.

7 DECEMBER 1941	SPRING 1942	APRIL 1942	4–7 JUNE 1942
Japan attacks the US naval base at Pearl Harbor, bringing America into the war. In the following weeks it also attacks British territories in the Far East.	Increasing merchant shipping losses to German U-boats put Britain's survival at stake	The Royal Air Force begins its systematic 'area bombing' of German cities	The US Navy gains a vital victory over the Japanese at the Battle of Midway, giving it naval superiority in the Pacific

IRENE FORSDYKE: BARRAGE BALLOON OPERATOR

High flier
Laura Knight's painting,
A Balloon Site, Coventry,
depicts the sort of work that
Irene and her crew were doing
LAURA KNIGHT, 1943. IWM ART LD 2750

During the Second World War, a complex web of large barrage balloons was flown over key target sites in Britain to force bombers to fly higher and so make their raids less accurate. In October 1941, Irene Forsdyke became one of the first women to be trained as a balloon operator.

It was tough work. Irene's crew was stationed on a slag heap in Sheffield, 'covered in black dust in dry weather, and black mud in wet'. Another time, they had to set up operations in a graveyard. Defending a target site also meant being stationed directly in the line of fire. Bombs fell all around and machine guns were trained on the crews from the skies as enemy planes attempted to disrupt the defences.

Bad weather brought its own dangers. Sudden gusts of wind could drag balloons from their moorings, sending thousands of feet of thick steel cable whipping around among the operators. One of Irene's friends broke both her legs, another her foot.

In May 1942, for example, there came the so-called 'Thousand Bomber Raid' on Cologne – the first of many mass attacks. That July, the United States Army Air Force lent its weight to the campaign, launching daytime raids to match the RAF's night-time work.

Between March and July 1943, British and American bombers fought the 'Battle of the Ruhr' and in July the RAF launched a series of devastating raids on Hamburg. Three quarters of the city was destroyed in the firestorm, a million people lost their homes, and 40,000 were killed.

By 1944, despite consistently heavy losses, the Allies had gained the upper hand in the skies. But debate continues on whether the raids, which eventually killed some 750,000 German civilians, had a decisive effect on either the economy or the morale of the enemy.

Defending the fatherland
Volunteer members of the *Luftschutz,*
the German civilian air defence
organisation, were issued with helmets
like this one from 1938 onwards.
IWM UNI 7977

AUGUST 1942
After a stalled offensive in the Soviet Union in December 1941 and a renewed push in spring 1942, the Germans reach the city of Stalingrad

NOVEMBER 1942
Britain wins its first major land victory over Germany at El Alamein (right). Fighting in North Africa continues until May 1943.
IWM E 18474

JANUARY 1943
A Soviet counter-offensive forces the Germans to surrender at Stalingrad. In July Germany is defeated at Kursk – its last offensive in the east.

WAR IN THE DESERT, WAR IN THE JUNGLE

In June 1940, Italy entered the war on Germany's side and in September invaded Egypt from Libya. Britain had to respond quickly; if the Suez Canal fell into enemy hands, it would cut off the country's vital trade and supply link to India and the Far East.

For three years, the British battled against Italian and then German forces, trading blows back and forth across the deserts of North Africa. The turning point came in July 1942 when they held back a German offensive at El Alamein, and then launched a successful attack of their own on the same spot three months later. The momentum generated by this victory eventually saw the fighting move back across the Mediterranean and on to Italian soil in the summer of 1943.

The war in North Africa had a character all of its own. It was man against man, but also man against desert – and each side developed respect for the efforts of the other to overcome this mutual enemy. There was almost an element of chivalry between the opposing forces – a chivalry that was all too lacking in the jungles of the Far East.

When Japan burst into the war in December 1941, it quickly captured a great deal of British territory in the Far East, including Hong Kong, Malaya, Singapore and Burma. By May 1942, it controlled much of Asia.

The efforts of British and Commonwealth troops to fight back were hampered by the terrible conditions – stifling heat, monsoon rains and tropical diseases – and by the fanaticism of the Japanese. It was a shock to face an enemy who preferred suicide to surrender – an attitude that reinforced the belief that the Japanese could not be beaten.

The spell was broken in 1944 when the Japanese invaded India. The reorganised British and Indian divisions mounted effective defensive actions at Kohima, Imphal and in the Arakan, and then began pushing the Japanese back – first out of India and then Burma. The war in the jungle was being won.

Life saver

Water was as vital as a gun to a soldier in the desert or jungle. This kit was issued to British and Commonwealth troops in the Far East to sterilise their drinking supply.
IWM SUR 71

SEPTEMBER 1943

After Allied landings in Sicily and on the Italian mainland, Italy surrenders to the Allies. The Germans continue to fight on Italian soil.

SPRING 1944

Japan invades India but by July is repelled by British and Indian troops (left)
IWM IB 291

6 JUNE 1944

The Allies land an invasion force in France. A week later, the Germans begin firing V-1 flying bombs at Britain.

*'And we've managed
to tell the world.
And we'll go on telling,
in the hope that their
future won't be our past.'*

Esther Brunstein, Holocaust survivor

Torn apart
A blue-grey striped jacket as worn by
inmates selected for slave labour at
the Majdanek concentration camp.
IWM UNI 11110

GENOCIDE

When the Nazis assumed power in Germany, they
began persecuting the country's Jewish population,
stripping them of their livelihoods and passing laws
to push them beyond the boundaries of society.
After the outbreak of war, persecution became
mass murder. Six million of the nine million Jews in
Europe were killed – one million of them children.

They were not the only victims. Gypsies (Roma and
Sinti), Soviet prisoners of war, non-Jewish Poles,
people with disabilities, homosexuals, Jehovah's
Witnesses and political opponents were all targeted
by the Nazis and their collaborators.

It was a murderous campaign that became gradually
more systematised. After war broke out, German
troops began rounding up the Jewish population
into squalid, overcrowded ghettos. Half a million
Jews died in ghettos from starvation and disease.

In the summer of 1941, as Hitler's troops marched
into the Soviet Union, specially organised murder
squads shot Jews and Communists behind the
front lines. Nearly one and a half million Jews are
estimated to have been killed in this way.

Over time a more efficient method was devised.
Jews across Europe were forced on to trains and
transported to specially constructed 'death camps'.
About one in five was kept alive for slave labour.
The rest were killed immediately in gas chambers.

AUGUST 1944	DECEMBER 1944	30 APRIL 1945	6 AUGUST 1945
The Red Army reaches the German border in the east. In September, US troops do the same in the west.	The Germans fail in an offensive in the Ardennes, which becomes known as the Battle of the Bulge	Hitler commits suicide in Berlin, as Soviet troops storm the city. On 8 May, the Western Allies declare Victory in Europe Day.	The first atomic bomb is dropped on Hiroshima. Japan surrenders on 14 August 1945.

IMPRESSIONS OF WAR

The British soldiers of the First World War were said to be 'lions led by donkeys'. Britain's lone stand against the Nazis in 1940 was the country's 'finest hour'. America should never have become embroiled in the Vietnam War. We all have our views on war — but how accurate are they and where do they come from? This Silo explores the ways in which our impressions of war are shaped — through the media, propaganda, popular culture, children's games and even through visits to museums like IWM North.

DID YOU KNOW?

People often talk about a 'lost generation' of British men killed during the First World War. In fact, 88 per cent of those who went off to fight came home.

We shall not forget (right)

The ex-servicemen organisation, Comrades of the Great War, was set up in 1917. In 1920 it amalgamated with two other groups to form the British Legion, and a year later the new organisation launched its first annual poppy appeal. It was part of a new form of remembrance in Britain that continues to colour our impression of the conflict even a century later.

IWM INS 5648

Early impressions

War — especially the Second World War — has long been a staple source of toys, games, books and comics for Britain's children, like this set of Airfix British Commandos. They often present a distorted view of the conflict — of 'goodies' and 'baddies', 'glorious victory' and 'heroic defeat'.

IWM EPH 3360

Forming opinion

Propaganda — the organised spreading of true and false information — is vital in shaping public attitudes to war. In the First World War the government used leaflets, posters, newspapers and film to get its message across. Radio played its part in the Second World War, and television has been used since. In September 1939, for example, families across Britain would have used radios like this one to listen to Prime Minister Neville Chamberlain telling the country that it was at war.

IWM COM 238

Finest hour

Civil Defence wardens wore helmets like this one during the Blitz of 1940. Objects of this type have become iconic of a period often referred to as Britain's 'finest hour' — as the country faced the Nazis alone after the fall of France. Yet, as this Silo explores, this view of the war is based more on myth than fact. Britain was not alone. It had the support of the Empire and Commonwealth, and between June 1940 and June 1941 a quarter of all its supplies from overseas were carried by the Norwegian Merchant Navy.

IWM UNI 444

LOOK OUT FOR...

- The 'Dead Man's Penny' — the nickname for the official next-of-kin memorial plaques sent to relatives of servicemen who died during the First World War.

- The photographs taken by George Rodger while covering the Second World War for *Life* magazine. Rodger was one of the first photographers to enter Bergen-Belsen concentration camp in April 1945.

- The Oscar awarded to *The True Glory*, 1945 Academy Awards winner of Best Documentary Feature. The imaginative production methods used in this film still influence documentary making to this day.

COLD WAR 1946–1989

The dropping of the atomic bomb on Hiroshima and Nagasaki brought the Second World War to a sudden end. The next forty years – covered in the fourth section of the Timeline – were dominated by fears that great arsenals of such weapons might be used once again.

The US and Soviet Union were unlikely allies in the Second World War, united by the threat posed by Nazi Germany but divided by the differences in their political systems and ways of life. As they advanced towards Berlin from west and east in the closing days of the war, each grew fearful of the other's plans, aims and military might.

This atmosphere of mutual mistrust soon turned into a tense stand-off that became known as the Cold War. Europe was divided into two rival military alliances – NATO led by the US, and the Warsaw Pact dominated by the Soviets. The battle lines for a new era of warfare had been drawn.

'From Stettin in the Baltic to Trieste in the Adriatic an iron curtain has descended across the continent.'

Winston Churchill, March 1946

Looming threat
The mushroom cloud generated during Britain's first test in May 1957 of a hydrogen bomb – even more powerful than the atom bomb. Britain was the third country after the US and the Soviet Union to gain such capability.
IWM GOV 9111

COLD WAR TIMELINE
The end of the Second World War did not bring peace. A new power struggle sprang up between the US and the Soviet Union, characterised by a series of indirect clashes around the globe. Britain's armed forces also saw action both at home and thousands of miles away overseas.

JUNE 1948
The Soviets block access to West Berlin to secure control of the entire city. The Western Allies fly in supplies eventually forcing the Soviets to back down.

OCTOBER 1949
Chinese Communists defeat the Chinese Nationalist Army and create a new communist state – the People's Republic of China

DIVIDED WORLD

The nature of the Cold War was partly defined by its weapons. The Soviet Union performed its first atomic bomb test in August 1949, and before long both sides had amassed nuclear arsenals more than capable of destroying the world.

The risks of a direct military confrontation were almost incalculable. Instead the two superpowers fought each other indirectly in a series of wars around the world — notably in Korea from 1950 to 1953, and in Vietnam from 1964 to 1975.

Only once did all-out nuclear war look like becoming a reality — in October 1962 when the US uncovered Soviet moves to site nuclear missiles in Cuba. The world held its breath for two weeks before both sides finally backed down.

Relations between east and west improved during the 1970s — in a period known as Détente. Treaties to limit each side's nuclear arsenals were signed in 1972 and then again in 1979, and the Helsinki Accords of 1975 settled many of the European border questions that had caused rancour since the end of the Second World War.

The decision by the Soviet Union in 1979 to invade Afghanistan put an end to this thaw. But while the Soviet Union remained a formidable military power, its economy — and that of its Warsaw Pact satellites — was falling behind.

By the end of the 1980s, this economic trouble had given rise to widespread political unrest. Finally, in 1989, the communist regimes in Poland and Hungary collapsed and the Soviet Union crumbled. The Cold War was over.

Dividing line

In 1961, the communist government in East Germany built a wall to divide its half of the city of Berlin from the sector governed by the western Allies. This piece of the wall was acquired by British military personnel after the fall of the Berlin Wall in 1989 — a powerful symbol of the end of the Cold War.
IWM EPH 675

JUNE 1950

Communist North Korea invades UN-backed South Korea. War follows (right) until a ceasefire is agreed three years later.
IWM MH 33028

AUGUST 1961

East Germany's communist government builds the Berlin Wall to stop its citizens leaving the city for the West

OCTOBER 1962

The US challenges the Soviet decision to site nuclear missiles in Cuba. The resulting crisis is the closest that the world has come to nuclear war.

DID YOU KNOW?

The Korean War that began in 1950 has still not formally come to an end. A ceasefire was agreed in 1953 but over 60 years later no peace treaty has yet been signed.

War of ideologies

The war in Vietnam was part of the wider Cold War, with the US providing military assistance to South Vietnam in its fight against communist forces in the North. These two posters illustrate the ideological side of the struggle. The example on the left accuses the communists of atrocities against civilians. The one on the right calls for 'American Imperialists' to get out of South Vietnam.

IWM PST 2518, IWM PST 2633

AUGUST 1964

An attack on two of its ships escalates US involvement in a war between South Vietnam and the communist North. The war lasts until 1975.

AUGUST 1968

Soviet-backed troops invade Czechoslovakia to overthrow leader Alexander Dubcek, who had tried to reform the communist government

APRIL 1969

British troops are sent to Northern Ireland to stop Protestant attacks on Catholics. They are soon targeted by Republican terrorists.

MAY 1972

The US and Soviet Union sign the Strategic Arms Limitation Treaty (SALT I), limiting the number of nuclear warheads in their respective arsenals

CHANGING BRITAIN

Britain's place in the world began to change after the Second World War. There were growing calls for independence from around the empire and British forces were employed to police the often difficult process of handing over power – in India, Palestine, Kenya and elsewhere.

The slow loss of its empire did nothing to help the country's economy, which had been hit hard by the war effort. Drained of resources, Britain was reduced to playing more of a supporting role as America assumed the lead in the west.

At home, there were other changes. Less than two months after leading his country to victory over Germany, Prime Minister Winston Churchill was voted out of office. The Conservative Party, which he led, was seen as the cause rather than the cure for the nation's social problems. In came a new Labour government and the introduction of the welfare state – the cornerstone of what was designed to be a new, fairer, more caring Britain.

Living conditions in the country gradually improved during the 1950s and 1960s and the make-up of society began to change. In May 1948, some 492 West Indian men and women disembarked at Tilbury Docks from the ship SS *Empire Windrush* to live and work in Britain. Their arrival marked the start of a period of post-war immigration which peaked in the late 1960s, laying the foundations for the multi-racial society we see today.

By the 1970s Britain had become more troubled – suffering the effects of a global economic recession and disturbed by violence on the streets of Northern Ireland. At the end of the decade a new Conservative government began to tackle

LINDA KITSON: WAR ARTIST IN THE FALKLANDS

In 1982, 37-year-old Linda Kitson became the first woman to accompany British troops to the front line as a war artist. She specialised in drawings made with conté crayon, which meant she could capture a scene in a matter of minutes. It was an invaluable skill given the speed at which the troops moved across the islands and the freezing conditions in which she had to work with fingers exposed. She was well looked after by the soldiers. One even made her a camouflage armband to hold the five drawing tools she used most often.

On route to war

Kitson (left) sailed for the Falklands on the QE2, which was used as a troopship during the conflict. Three drawings of the crossing are exhibited in the displays.

MARY EVANS PICTURE LIBRARY/DAVID KIRBY, IWM ART 15530 3

OCTOBER 1973

Egypt and Syria attack Israel during the Jewish festival of Yom Kippur, but fail in their attempt to regain territory lost in earlier wars in 1956 and 1967

DECEMBER 1979

Soviet troops invade Afghanistan to install a pro-Moscow regime. They remain in the country until 1989.

AUGUST 1980

A new union of Polish shipyard workers strikes to defy the communist government – part of a wider bid for political freedom in Eastern Europe

APRIL 1982

Argentina invades the Falklands. Britain retakes the islands in June. The lives of 253 Britons and 655 Argentinians are lost.

the situation by dismantling the country's state-owned industries in favour of a free market service economy. Clashes between striking workers and the authorities were all too common.

In April 1982, Britain went to war to reclaim the distant Falkland Islands from invading Argentinian forces. It had the appearance of an old-fashioned war, often involving hand-to-hand combat between the two sets of soldiers.

But Britain also remained committed to the more modern manoeuvrings of the Cold War. In 1983, it allowed US missiles to be based on its soil – a controversial decision that raised renewed fears of nuclear armageddon. Few expected then that the Cold War would be over by the end of the decade.

Troubling sight

The Northern Ireland Troubles began in 1968 with violent clashes between those wanting to remain within the United Kingdom and those who wanted to become part of the Irish Republic. The following year British troops were sent to police the streets. For 30 years armed soldiers were an everyday sight in this part of the United Kingdom.

IWM TR 32956

NOVEMBER 1983

US cruise and Pershing missiles arrive at bases in Europe, sparking fierce local protests. The missiles remain until 1991.

NOVEMBER 1985

US President Ronald Reagan and Soviet leader Mikhail Gorbachev meet for the first time. At two later summits they agree to cut their nuclear arsenals.

NOVEMBER 1989

After communist regimes collapse in Poland and Hungary, citizens tear down the Berlin Wall (left) – the symbolic end of the Cold War   IWM HU 73009

EMPIRE, COMMONWEALTH AND WAR

The Allied victories in the First and Second World Wars owed a great deal to the contribution of the peoples who made up the British Empire and Commonwealth. Eight million fought in the wars, and countless more worked to provide vital supplies, armaments and raw materials. This Silo explores the effort and sacrifice involved and looks at how war has changed the relationship between the British Empire, the Commonwealth and Britain.

> *'The fame of the Garwhals is now higher than the skies.'*
>
> *Bigya Singh of the Indian Garwhal Brigade writing home from the Western Front in March 1915*

Island effort (right)

Nearly 10,000 West Indian men and over 600 West Indian women served during the Second World War – most in the Royal Air Force. Since German U-boats were known to be operating in the Caribbean, many West Indians also joined units such as the Barbados Volunteer Force, set up to defend their islands.

IWM INS 4945

Canadian contribution

Canada's armed forces played a major role during Operation Overlord – the invasion of north west Europe in June 1944. By the end of July, every unit of the Canadian Army Overseas was in action in Europe, including the 17th Duke of York Royal Canadian Hussars, whose insignia is on display in the Silo.

IWM INS 5655

ANZAC sacrifice

In April 1915 thousands of men from the Australian and New Zealand Army Corps (ANZAC) were landed at Gallipoli in a disastrous attempt to knock Turkey out of the war. By January 1916, they had been evacuated after months of bloody fighting. This Turkish dagger was taken from a captured position by an Australian soldier.

IWM WEA 793

World at war

On 31 October 1914, Sepoy (Private) Khudadad Khan of the Indian Army kept his machine gun in action after the rest of his section had been killed during a German attack. He was later awarded the Victoria Cross for his actions. His traditional knife (known as a 'kukri') can be seen in the displays.

IWM VC 694

LOOK OUT FOR...

- The silkworm gut used by the men of the Indian Army for stitching up wounds in the Second World War.

- The bottle of Australian wine dating back to the Second World War.

- The imitation wristwatch made for one of the leaders of the Mau Mau insurgency against British rule in Kenya.

Fight for independence

After the Second World War, many people in Britain's Empire and Commonwealth demanded independence for their countries – calls which sometimes resulted in violence. In Kenya, British troops were brought in to defeat what became known as the Mau Mau insurgency. Mau Mau fighters had access to few firearms, so some chose to make their own – such as the pistol on display in the Silo.

IWM FIR 10612

SCIENCE, TECHNOLOGY AND WAR

Political and military leaders have always tried to harness the power of science and technology to gain an edge in war. Weapons have become more powerful, defence systems more ingenious and communications ever more speedy and reliable. This Silo looks at the scientific and medical advances made as a result of war — and examines their consequences both positive and negative.

Winged messengers (above)
In theory soldiers in the First World War could communicate via the relatively new technologies of telephone and radio. In practice telephone wires were easily severed and radios were too cumbersome. In many cases, pigeons were used to send messages. This collapsible pigeon box was used by the Germans in the First World War.
IWM COM 7

Jet power

Before the Second World War Britain and Germany raced to develop faster fighter aircraft to defend themselves from bomber attack. In 1944, the British brought the Gloster Meteor into service – a model of which is on display in the Silo. Like the German Messerschmitt 262, it was powered by a jet engine – a revolution in military and civil aviation.
IWM MOD 813

Defensive measures

In the run-up to the Second World War both sides feared that enemy aircraft might employ poison gas attacks against civilians. Citizens were issued with protective gear developed during the First World War when poison gas was first used on the front line. The respirator shown here was designed for use by a baby.
IWM EQU 2835

DID YOU KNOW?

War fuels medical advances. In 1914, 80 per cent of gunshot wounds involving fractures led to amputation. By 1918, the rate had fallen to seven per cent.

Shadow of the bomb

The devastation unleashed by the atomic bomb in 1945 shocked the world. After the Second World War, there came the even greater threat of the nuclear bomb – but the same technology was also applied to generate electricity. In the Silo, you can see this British WE 177 nuclear bomb, which remained in service until 1998.
IWM MUN 4851

LOOK OUT FOR...

- The First World War whistle used by British officers to signal the order to 'go over the top' and begin the advance across no-man's land towards enemy lines.

- The posters warning British soldiers in the Second World War about the dangers of contracting sexually transmitted diseases.

- The cup recovered from the ruins of Hiroshima by a British officer in the months after the dropping of the atomic bomb.

INTO A NEW CENTURY 1990–PRESENT

The final section of the Timeline starts from the end of the Cold War and brings you to the present day. It looks at the ways in which the nature of war has changed – and the ways in which it remains all too familiar.

The collapse of communism was heralded by many as the beginning of a new, better era. Capitalism and democracy had triumphed. Superpower no longer stood against superpower, nuclear arsenal against nuclear arsenal. The threat of a cataclysmic Third World War seemed to be passing.

But the fall of the Soviet Union left a political vacuum in Eastern Europe and the Balkans, which soon led to new conflict. Meanwhile, American troops were being deployed to the Middle East – a region that has since played a central role in the story of war in the new century.

Field of fire
A soldier of 1st Battalion, The Irish Guards keeps a watch on enemy positions as Royal Engineers cap a burning oil well within the city of Basra in Iraq, 3 April 2003.
IWM OP-TELIC-03-010-34-009

'As the world looks back to nine decades of war, of strife, of suspicion, let us also look forward – to a new century of peace, freedom and prosperity.'

US President George H W Bush, January 1990

INTO A NEW CENTURY TIMELINE
War continues to shape the lives of people around the world – fired by age-old issues of ethnicity, culture and religion. But the manner in which it is waged has changed – as the events of the recent past demonstrate.

JANUARY 1991
An international coalition goes to war to liberate Kuwait from its Iraqi invaders. The ground war lasts 100 hours and the Iraqis are expelled.

JUNE 1991
Following communism's collapse, politicians try to divide Yugoslavia into ethnically 'pure' states, sparking a bloody war in the region

CHANGING WARFARE

The Gulf War of 1991 was beamed directly into living rooms around the world. Viewers watched as sophisticated 'smart' bombs appeared to hit their targets with pinpoint accuracy, and coalition ground forces took just 100 hours to expel Iraqi troops from Kuwait. It looked like a campaign waged with surgical precision but its repercussions were less clear. For one thing, Iraqi dictator Saddam Hussein remained in power and would prove to be a major reason for the outbreak of another war in the region in 2003.

The succession of wars in the former Yugoslavia – in Slovenia, Croatia, Bosnia-Herzegovina, Kosovo and Macedonia – proved to be the bloodiest in Europe since the Second World War. Battle lines were drawn according to ethnicity, with neighbour turning against neighbour and millions forced to leave their homes. Ethnicity also lay at the heart of the 100-day campaign of terror waged in 1994 by Hutu militias against the Tutsis in Rwanda. Some 800,000 Tutsis were killed in a genocide that shocked the world.

Sci-fi inspiration

This helmet, its design apparently influenced by the popular 1977 science fiction film *Star Wars*, was issued to members of Saddam Hussein's most fanatic of supporters, the *Fedayeen Saddam* (Saddam's Martyrs). It was of little worth in terms of personal protection.

IWM UNI 13695

56

Colonial combat

The web of war is often complex. This automatic light machine gun was captured by British forces during the 1991 Gulf War. Some of its parts are thought to have come from the former state of Yugoslavia – itself ravaged by war before the turn of the century.

IWM FIR 10395

APRIL–JULY 1994	APRIL 1994	APRIL 1998	FEBRUARY 2000
Hutu militias butcher 800,000 Tutsis in a 100-day reign of terror in Rwanda that ends with the overthrow of the Hutu government by the Rwandan Patriotic Front	Apartheid – the forced segregation of people according to the colour of their skin – comes to an end in South Africa after 46 years	The British and Irish governments sign the Good Friday Agreement creating a political framework to resolve the troubles in Northern Ireland	President Robert Mugabe begins a campaign of violence and starvation against political opponents in Zimbabwe

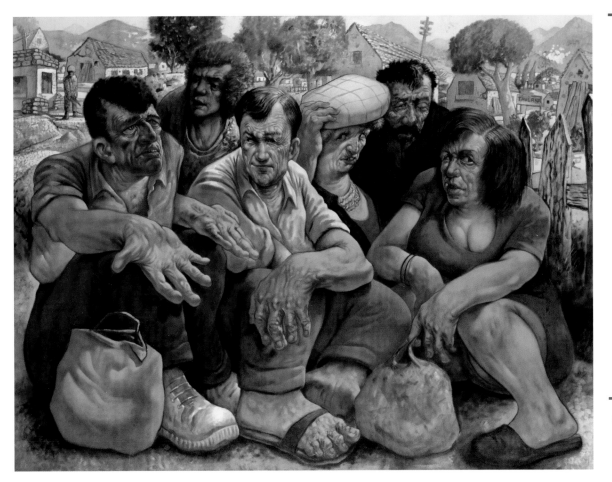

Human cost

Cleansed, 1994 by Peter Howson. Howson travelled to Bosnia as an official war artist. His painting, which is on display in the Main Exhibition Space, shows a group of Muslim refugees who have been driven from their homes at gunpoint by Croatians.

IWM ART 16521

DID YOU KNOW?

The UK's involvement in Iraq from 2003 to 2011 was codenamed Operation Telic. Service personnel joked that it stood for 'Tell Everyone Leave Is Cancelled'.

SEPTEMBER 2001

Terrorists crash hijacked planes into the World Trade Center and the Pentagon. A month later the US leads an invasion of Afghanistan.

FEBRUARY 2003

The Sudanese government arms a militia, the *Janjaweed*, to pursue a policy of ethnic cleansing in Darfur. Some 400,000 are killed and 2.5 million become refugees.

MARCH 2003

Coalition forces, led by the US, launch a controversial invasion of Iraq (left) and oust its leader Saddam Hussein

Terrorists crash United Airlines Flight 175 into the South Tower of the World Trade Center at 9.03am on 11 September 2001 – sparking a new 'war on terror'.

© CARMEN TAYLOR/AP/PA

CHANGING WARFARE CONTINUES

After the new century dawned, the nature of warfare changed again. On 11 September 2001, America, the world's great military superpower, was attacked on its own soil. The weapons were hijacked planes. Two were crashed into the World Trade Center and one into the Pentagon. A fourth crashed in Pennsylvania. Thousands were killed. The attack came not from a rival superpower or an enemy state but from a shadowy terrorist group called al-Qaeda, which believed that America posed a threat to the Islamic world.

America's response was to declare a 'war on terror' and to fight for a victory that remains hard to define. It quickly led to the invasion of Afghanistan, where the al-Qaeda terrorists were believed to be based.

Then came the Iraq War of 2003, after links were drawn between Saddam Hussein and global terrorism. The effects of these conflicts continue to be felt around the world today.

> ### 'We must reaffirm that the United States is not and never will be at war with Islam.'
>
> **US President Barack Obama, May 2011**

LIEUTENANT SIMON CUPPLES: DECORATED FOR BRAVERY

In 2007, 25-year-old Lieutenant Simon Cupples was serving in Afghanistan with the 2nd Battalion, The Mercian Regiment. On 7 September his company headed out on a mission to clear and destroy a Taliban position. They were within 30 metres of their target when they came under heavy machine gun fire. Four of the seven-man section were hit.

For the next three hours Lieutenant Cupples repeatedly risked his life to help his wounded comrades, at one point crawling to within 15 metres of the Taliban position. He was later awarded the Conspicuous Gallantry Cross for his actions – joining a group of only a few dozen other members of the armed forces to receive the award since its creation in 1993.

Conspicuous gallantry
Lieutenant Cupples (left) loaned his Conspicuous Gallantry Cross to IWM North in 2009. It is on display in this section of the Timeline.
SIMON CUPPLES

---

7 JULY 2005
Islamist suicide bombers attack London's transport system (right) during rush hour – apparently motivated by Britain's military action in Iraq and elsewhere
NOEL AND ROBERT MCLEOD   HU 93645

DECEMBER 2008
Amid ongoing conflict between Israel and Palestine, Israel opens a three-week attack on Gaza. Over a thousand Palestinians are killed.

2 MAY 2011
Al-Qaeda leader Osama Bin Laden is traced and killed in Pakistan by US Special Forces

LEGACY OF WAR

Wars can end in victory, defeat or stalemate. But the effects of war can linger for years to come — on individuals, their relatives, their communities and their countries. This Silo explores what happens when war ends and people on all sides begin the difficult task of piecing together their shattered lives.

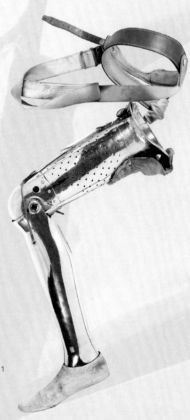

DID YOU KNOW?
Landmines left behind after wars and conflicts kill or maim someone, somewhere in the world, every 22 minutes.

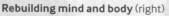

Rebuilding mind and body (right)
Few servicemen return from war completely unscarred. Most carry some physical, mental or emotional trauma with lasting effects on the rest of their lives. Private G H Hobday of the Oxfordshire and Buckinghamshire Light Infantry, for example, lost a leg in the Second World War. He used this artificial limb until his death in 1998, aged 81.

 IWM SUR 511

From arms to art

After a long civil war came to an end in Mozambique in 1992, millions of weapons remained hidden away. In one project, people were encouraged to exchange their weapons for tools. Artists then used fragments of the destroyed weapons to create works of art, such as this crocodile made from machine gun cartridge belts.

IWM EPH 3503

'*The bonds of family had been broken (when I came home). I was a totally different person.*'

Herminio Martinez, Spanish Civil War evacuee during the 1930s

Returning to civilian life

Occupational therapy has long played a part in the rehabilitation of severely injured soldiers. It keeps men busy as they recover and helps prepare them for finding practical civilian work. This wooden fretwork figure of a Red Cross Voluntary Aid Detachment nurse was made by a wounded serviceman in Malta during the First World War.

IWM EPH 3252

Crisis management

In the immediate aftermath of war, it often falls to governments, aid organisations and charities to provide food and shelter for the civilian population. This tin of canned beef was sent to Kosovo after the crisis there at the end of the twentieth century.

IWM EPH 3301

LOOK OUT FOR...

- The rose petals taken as a keepsake from the grave of Lance Corporal Ernest Nicholson, who was killed near Ypres in 1917.

- The letter written by Guy Nightingale to his mother describing his experience of the landings at Gallipoli in 1915. In 1934, unable to come to terms with his memories, Guy took his life.

- The tailfin of a German incendiary bomb recovered from a garden in Manchester. The Luftwaffe raids of 1940 and 1941 meant that the city centre had to be substantially rebuilt.

IWM NORTH AND YOU

If you have enjoyed your visit to IWM North, there are several ways to extend that experience — both on the day and on future occasions — and to share it with family, friends or colleagues.

OPENING HOURS

IWM North is open daily 10am – 5pm
Last Admission 30 minutes before closing
Closed 24, 25, 26 December

KEEP IN TOUCH

Sign up for our eNews, packed with information about upcoming exhibitions, events and stories inspired by our world-renowned collection: **iwm.org.uk/eNews**. Post, tweet or snap your IWM experience with us on Twitter via **@IWMNorth** or on Instagram via **ImperialWarMuseums** using **#IWMNorth**, or find us on Facebook.

SHOPPING

IWM North's shop provides a wide range of inspiring gifts, books, clothing and accessories, vintage posters, stationery, homeware, toys and souvenirs - all inspired by our collections and the stories they tell. You can also shop online at **iwmshop.org.uk**

FAMILY ACTIVITIES, SCHOOLS AND LEARNING

We offer a wide range of activities and resources for schools, families and the general public. These include interactive sessions, performances, talks, workshops, conferences and online resources. Visit **iwm.org.uk/visits/iwm-north/groups and iwm. org.uk/whats-on**

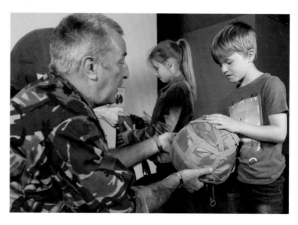

VOLUNTEERING

We are privileged to have volunteers support IWM in a variety of roles and we value their expertise, knowledge and dedication. Are you ready to be a part of our story? To find out more, and to search and apply for volunteer vacancies, please visit **iwm.org.uk/volunteer**

CAFÉ

The IWM North Café, located on the ground floor, opens daily from 10am offering a delicious selection of homemade, seasonal food with a local influence including deli sandwiches, salads, cakes and pastries.

SUPPORT US

IWM North explores the impact of war on everyone involved. Our dynamic exhibitions and use of digital media engage people of all ages from across our community with the issues of war and conflict. IWM is a charity and we rely on the generous support of our visitors, major donors, companies and charitable trusts. Help us to care for and display our collections, and to inspire visitors of all ages to build an understanding of war and conflict, and how these events shape our world.

You can support us by making a donation at **iwm.org.uk/corporate/support-us** or by texting **IWMN00 £5** to **70070**. To learn more about the ways you can support us please call **020 7416 5140**.

MEMBERSHIP

Joining us as a member is a great way to support our work whilst enjoying many benefits for you and your family. These include free entry to all our branches (HMS *Belfast*, Churchill War Rooms and IWM Duxford all charge a general admission fee), and discounts in IWM restaurants, cafés and shops. As a charity we depend on our members' support to enable the stories of those impacted by conflict to continue to be told from one generation to the next, and to ensure that our world-leading collection and historically important sites are protected for the future. We couldn't do it without the moral and financial support of our members.

For full details on how you can become a member and make a difference, please speak to a member of staff or a volunteer, or **visit iwm.org.uk/membership**

MEETINGS AND EVENTS

IWM North are the only museum in the UK to hold Food for the Brain Accreditation – all delegate menus are created to support mental health, well-being, concentration and performance.

Our new WaterShard event rooms are perfect for conferences, meetings and small dinners. The space holds up to 120 theatre-style or 80 cabaret, and can be split for smaller meetings.

The Main Exhibition Space, with its creative lighting and 360 HD digital projection wallpapers, provides a stunning backdrop to your event. The space is perfect for Christmas parties, awards dinners and summer parties, with up to 300 seated banqueting-style or up to 650 receptions. For more intimate events, we have space under our spectacular Harrier Jump Jet – perfect for dinners up to 60, or receptions of 260.

ABOUT IWM

IWM is a global authority on conflict and its impact in Britain and its former Empire and Commonwealth, from the First World War to the present day and beyond. We collect objects and stories that give an insight into people's experiences of war and we preserve them for future generations. By telling these stories on our website – **iwm.org.uk** – and across our five branches, we aim to help people understand why we go to war and the effect that conflict has on people's lives. As a charity, we rely on admission fees, our cafés, sales in our shops (including **iwmshop.org.uk**) and donations to continue our work and to ensure that the stories of those who have lived, fought and died in conflicts since 1914 continue to be heard.

IWM LONDON

In Summer 2014, **IWM London** re-opened with a transformed new atrium, designed by architects Foster + Partners, as well as ground-breaking new First World War Galleries to mark the 100 year anniversary of the start of the war. The 'new' IWM London reveals more of IWM's unique collections, telling important stories of people's experiences of war and conflict up to the present day, including how conflict has divided communities in places such as Ireland, Iraq and Afghanistan.

Lambeth Road, London SE1 6HZ.

IWM DUXFORD

Set within the best-preserved Second World War airfield in Europe, **IWM Duxford** is a vibrant museum that marries its fascinating past with award-winning interactive exhibitions, working hangars and an exciting programme of events. Home to an impressive collection of over 200 aircraft as well as tanks, military vehicles and boats, discover the fascinating stories behind the machines that changed our lives forever and the impact they had on the development of future technology.

Cambridgeshire, CB22 4QR.

CHURCHILL WAR ROOMS

Inside **Churchill War Rooms** lie the original Cabinet War Rooms – the secret underground bunker which sheltered Churchill and his staff during the Second World War. Explore the historic rooms, including the Map Room where the books and charts are exactly where they were left when the door was locked in 1945. Discover the stories of those who worked underground as London was bombed above them, and explore the life and legacy of Winston Churchill in the Churchill Museum.

Clive Steps, King Charles Street, London SW1A 2AQ.

HMS BELFAST

HMS *Belfast* is the most significant surviving Second World War Royal Navy warship, with a history that extends to the Cold War, Korea and beyond. Once home to a crew of up to 950 men, HMS *Belfast* tells the stories of those who lived on board this warship. Explore nine decks of seafaring history including the machines in the Engine Room that powered her across the world. Hear the sailors' battle stories and take control of a fleet in the Operations Room.

The Queen's Walk, London SE1 2JH.

For information relating to all IWM branches, please call **020 7416 5000**, or go to the website: **iwm.org.uk**